Citizenship by Investment:
Information on many nations including the United States

John Stuart Watkins

Table of Contents

Title page   1
Table of contents   2
John Stuart Watkins is not an attorney   3
Citizenship by Investment or by Residency   4
The U.S. Green Card Through Investment   5
U.S. Citizenship through Naturalization   6
Bulgarian Citizenship Act of 2013   7
Caribbean Islands; Antigua and Barbados   8
St. Lucia is an English-speaking country   9
Schenegen States Map   10
Hungary information   11
Dominican Republic information   12
Cyprus   13
St. Kitts   14
Grenada Citizenship   15
Portugal's Residency Program   16
Italy   17
Malta   18
CNN Report   19
Turkey   20
Canada   21
Australia   22
Germany   23
France   24
Greece   25
Spain   26
New Zeland   27
Mexico   28
Costa Rica   29
RAISE ACT   30
John Stuart Watkins resume 2017   31
Stuart Watkins published eight books   32

John Stuart Watkins is not an attorney and although he has spent three years researching the information in this book, times have changed, rules have changed, nation's laws have changed, and it is up to the person interested in buying citizenship in any of the nations mentioned in this book to check on the current laws, rules, and regulations.

Hire an attorney knowledgeable in the field to protect your interests before you invest any money in any of the nations that are offering citizenship for investment.

There are real estate agents in the United States who may be able to help persons interested in gaining citizenship in the United States, and their experience and expertise should be verified before making any commitments.

John Stuart Watkins is a licensed real estate agent in the State of Arizona. He is knowledgeable, but not an expert in any citizenship program in other nations, but has some helpful information on the current programs in the United States of America and other nations that can lead to citizenship.

Citizenship in the United States may not be bought, but a visa program leading to citizenship is currently available.

It is dedicated to all citizens of all nations seeking to better their life or living conditions.

Citizenship by Investment or Citizenship by Residency

There are benefits and/or drawbacks to both programs
Which is best for you?

Look into the various programs offered by various nations.
Seek legal counsel.

Salesmen and women want to make a sale. Make sure the information you receive actually suits your needs.

You may only need visa privileges to travel from nation to nation with few or no restrictions.

You may need a safe haven to place your cash in the event of upheaval in the nation where you reside, or in world events that are not in your favor.

You may want to actually live in another nation and want to understand the citizenship requirements of that nation.

You may want to reside in a nation part time, and still remain a citizen in the nation where you currently reside.

This book is a guide to citizenship in various nations and is not a legal reference. Do your own due diligence, or hire those who can do your research for you.

The United States Citizenship and Immigration Services have a Green Card Through Investment program that can lead to citizenship.

In short, an investor (and their spouses and unmarried children under the age of 21) making an investment of $1,000,000, or at least $500,000, in certain areas of the United States may be granted conditional permanent residence to the individual.

The spouse and unmarried children under the age of 21 may be included in the immigration petition.

Go to this website:

http://www.uscis.gov/green-card-through-job/green-card-through-investment

Remember that rules change and a current copy is a must.

Have your attorney read section 203(b)(5) of the Immigration and Nationality Act (INA) 8 U.S.C. 1153 (b)(5)

If you buy a business it must create at least ten new jobs directly or indirectly. This program was intended to cause job growth in underdeveloped regions of the U.S.

It was used to help build a new hospital in Green Valley near Tucson, Arizona. It has been used to buy condominiums in major U. S. cities. So, check it out.

U.S. Citizenship through Naturalization

To file:
you must be at least 18 years old, be able to read, write, and speak English, and be a person of good character.

There is a ten-step naturalization process including the determination that you are eligible to become a U.S. Citizen.

You have to prepare and submit form N-400, which is the application for naturalization. You also will take the U.S. Naturalization Test and then have a personal interview. Resources to prepare for the Naturalization Test:

100 Civics Questions and Answers
Naturalization Test Study Materials
Naturalization Self-Test

You can apply for a Certificate of Citizenship if you were born abroad to U.S. parents and they did not obtain a Consular Report of Birth Abroad.

Dual Citizenship or Nationality
A person may be a citizen of the United States and another country. (Hire an attorney to confirm and answer questions.)
Bulgarian Citizenship Act of 2013

You can become a resident by buying a government bond and holding it for five years at no interest. Today, it will cost about E511,292, but this amount may have changed, so it will have to be confirmed. If you double this amount, you can apply for their fast tract program by completing one year of permanent residency and then you can apply for citizenship.

By paying an additional E 100,000 you can get permanent residency in six months and apply for full citizenship in two years.

This program can be financed. There are no language requirements. You do not have to renounce your current residence. Bulgaria is a member of NATO and a member of the EU.

Bulgarian Citizenship Act of 2013

You can become a resident by buying a government bond and holding it for five years at no interest.

Today, it will cost about EUR 511,292, but this amount may have changed, so it will have to be confirmed by you.

If you double this amount, you can apply for their fast tract program by completing one year of permanent residency and then you can apply for citizenship.

By paying an additional EUR 100,000 you can get permanent residency in six months and apply for full citizenship in two years.

This program can be financed.

There are no language requirements.

You do not have to renounce your current residence.

Bulgaria is a member of NATO and a member of the EU.

The Caribbean Islands have two currently popular second citizenship programs offered by Antigua and Barbados.

Each require an investment of $250,000 US.
These island nations offer full citizenship and a British Commonwealth passport. This can be obtained in three months, and it is renewable every five years. Once the applicant is accepted, he or she will be granted lifetime citizenship.

No taxes. Dependents over sixty-five and children under twenty-five may be included.

The United Kingdom, Canada, Australia, Schenegen States, and about one hundred thirty countries are Visa-free, or Visa-on-arrival. The Antigua and Barbuda Investment Authority attracts foreign investment into their citizenship program.

You can make a cash donation to the National Development Fund which is sent directly to an escrow account managed by the CIU which invest in a freehold property with title deed, or fractional share in properties such as hotel shares, or land.

Investments start at $250,000 for the National Development Fund. This program may not still be available. Check it out. For the real estate option it takes $400,000.

Iranian and Iraq nationals are now being accepted in the Citizenship by investment program whereas they were not previously allowed.

St. Lucia is an English-speaking country.

It offers visa-free travel to 125 countries such as the United Kingdom, Schengen States, Singapore and Hong Kong.

There is a three-month processing time and a requirement for an investment of $100,000 for one person, $165,000 for the applicant and spouse, or $190,000 for a family of four.

There are tax benefits and no residency requirements. Some nations require a person to live there for a minimum period of time during the year.

I was told the beaches and resorts are top notch.

Schenegen States Map

Austria	Belgium	Czech Republic
Estonia	Finland	France
Greece	Hungary	Iceland
Latvia	Lithuania	Luxembourg
Netherlands	Norway	Poland

You will see references to this list throughout this book.

Hungary information:

You can own a visa free pass to all the Schenegen States.
You have an option to reside in an European nation.
You do not need to relocate to Hungary.
You do not have to visit Hungary.

You can apply without visiting Hungary, but the visit to Hungary will be pleasant and worth the time if you are interested in history. I have been there and loved all I saw.

Your family could become residents in two months. Check out the requirements to get all the details.

You have to invest E300,000 into a government bond.
The investment has to stay for five years.
After five years you will get a complete refund of your investment. (No interest.)

For each family member it will cost E125,000, but wait, there is also a government fee of E60,000 per family member.

Hungary is a part of the Schengen Area.

Hungary may cancel this program and you need to check to see if it is still available.

Contact the Hungarian Embassy to confirm.

Dominican Republic Information:

A Second Citizenship in the Dominica Republic in the Caribbean Islands will allow visa-free travel to about 120 countries.

You can travel to all the Schengen States and the United Kingdom.

If business is of interest to you, you may be able to establish a business in the middle east, as well as applying for residency.

Wait!

There is no inheritance tax. There is no death tax. There is no real estate tax. There is no worldwide income tax.

It will cost $100,000 for one applicant. It can be a donation or investment. You can maintain your current citizenship and do not have to relocate here.

The process could take three months.

Cyprus

Cyprus offers a second citizenship program and it could be granted within three months.

For E two million invested in a Cypriot business or real estate you can have an EU passport.

You will have the same rights as a natural born citizen.

There is a low corporate tax.

You get a 8% return on your real estate investment.

You have visa-free travel to over 155 countries. (check to see which ones are included.)

You can live or work in any of the current EU nations. (28?)

You have free trade within the EU.

St. Kitts

If this program is still available, and it is up to you to confirm, you have to invest $350,000 in a government approved real estate project.

There are additional legal fees and government fees.

Some Chinese have bought $700,000 homes in St. Kitts so they can travel internationally with little difficulty.

St. Kitts is one of a number of Caribbean islands that have different laws. Each island has its own government.

St. Kitts is one of those islands offering an economic citizenship program.

St. Kitts and Nevis started their citizenship program via investment in 1984. You could make a cash donation to the Sugar Industry Diversification foundation or invest in real estate approved by the government.

You were guaranteed a 100% return of your investment if you invested in real estate.

For a real estate investment, it required $400,000.
For the donation program, it required $250,000.

Both St. Kitts and Nevis have no direct personal taxes. They do not tax income earned outside of these nations.

Once again, you must check to see if these programs are currently available.

Grenada Citizenship

Lifetime citizenship is granted and it may not be revoked.

If you have $350,000 to invest in the Island Transformation Fund, after gaining permanent residency, it can be resold after five years. This program was proposed and you must confirm it is available.

You do not have to travel to Grenada while you apply for citizenship and your home country will not be made aware of your citizenship in Grenada.

You have access to about 100 countries. You have worldwide tax exemption. No visa is required.

Citizenship includes your children under 25 and dependents over 65.

Portugal's Residency Program

There is a minimum real estate investment of E350,000 in Lisbon or The Algarve.

There is a residency period of six years at the end of which any family member can apply for citizenship.

No visa is needed to have access to any Schenegen Nation, after citizenship has been granted.

You must spend one week each year in Portugal during the six years residency.

Portuguese is the national language.

The main religion is Roman Catholic.

Investors are guaranteed 100% return on their investment if they invest in real estate.

The real estate can be commercial or residential.

Italy

If you are applying for Italian Dual Citizenship, all U.S. documents require an Apostille and must be translated to Italian.

Go to their Italian Dual Citizenship Section and select the situation that best applies to you.

All birth, marriage and death certificates for all your family members (including your children under the age of 18, because they will acquire dual citizenship with you) in a direct line between you and your Italian ancestor must bear an Apostille and be translated into Italian.

These documents do not have to be translated into Italian:

Birth and death certificates for the spouses of your Italian ancestors.

U.S. Certificate of Naturalization or any statement releasing information on the naturalization status of the interested party.

All Apostilles

Your application and cover letter.

(Hire an attorney to assist you so there are no mistakes.)

Malta

Malta has no language requirements and it only requires EUR 30,000 for the main applicant.

You have to own a real estate purchase for five years and invest EUR 320,000 (EUR 270,000-Gozo/South of Malta)

Or

You may lease EUR 12,000 per year (EUR 10,000-Gozo/South of Malta.

Or

You may choose to invest EUR 250,000 in government approved bonds or stocks and hold them for five years.

There are additional fees for legal and application expenses.

According to a CNNMoney analysis of U.S. government data they report that the Chinese account for 80% of the U.S. immigrant investor program.

American Realtors should hone up on this market.

Turkey

Buy a property worth at least $1,000,000 that creates at least 100 jobs and Turkey will offer you citizenship.

Turkey allows dual citizenship.

You must be an adult, have lived in Turkey for 5 years, or 3 years if you marry a Turkish national, have no criminal record, be in good health, and speak the Turkish language.

Canada

Canada allows dual citizenship.
You pledge allegiance to both countries.
You have benefits in both countries.
You can vote in both countries.

You must live in Canada for 4 years and physically be in Canada 183 days each of those 4 years.

You cannot be under investigation for fraud or immigration reasons to become a citizen.

First, apply for a tourist visa. After 6 months you will need a work permit or school permit, or marry a Canadian.

Then actually move to Canada and get your Permanent Resident Card, or your "Maple Leaf Card," as some refer to the permanent card.

Stay in Canada for at least 1,460 days out of the past 4 years. Speak French or English. You will have to pass an oral test. Have no criminal record, nor be a security risk.

Download the Canadian Citizen Application Form from their website. Fill it our correctly or it will be returned. Pay the application fees in Canadian currency.

Fill out Form IMM5401.

When approved, appear for the citizenship oath.

Australia

Live there for 4 years.

You must have English language skills in listening, speaking, writing, and reading.

You will be tested.

Pledge allegiance to Australia.

Permanent Resident:

Skilled Independent Visa

Skilled Nomination Scheme

Employer Nomination Scheme

Regional Sponsored Scheme

Business Innovation Scheme

Business Talent Scheme

Resident Return Scheme

(Scheme means plan or program.)

Germany

Germany, no matter one's ethnicity, gives the German passport holder a "global citizen" according to one publication.

It makes one a member of the fourth largest economy in the world.

You have access to about 177 nations. This may have changed as world politics also change.

There is no minimum residency requirement.

Your passport is good for ten years and is renewable for your lifetime.

You do have to have some money and economic stability.

You must invest at least one million dollars in a German business that leads to hiring ten German citizens. It can be a new business or an existing business.

If you qualify, you then have all the rights of a German citizen.

Paperwork needed:

You must have a current passport.

You must have documents that show you intend to reside in Germany.

You must have health insurance for at least 30,000.

Two passport photos are required.

You must have sufficient funds to support yourself.

Have all documents such as birth certificates and marriage certificates for your family and dependents.

Welcome to Germany.

France

There is an Investor Program, but not for citizenship. It allows business persons to receive a 10-year economic residency permit. The investment must be long-term and not a speculative investment.

There is a requirement of a minimum of E 10,000,000 dollar investment.

You can invest through 30% ownership in a corporation, and must be able to prove ownership of at least 30% of the company shares.

You have access to the Schenegen Countries, which are currently about 127.

The economic residency permit is good for 10 years.

Your wife and children will have a French visa with no additional investment.

After 3 years of permanent residency in France, you can apply for citizenship, and there are no requirements that you know the language or special professional skills.

It may take two months or longer for the process to be completed.

Greece

Greece has a Residency and Citizenship program.

There is a Residency Program if you buy real estate property in Greece valued at least E 250,000.

The property must be a 2 or 3 bedroom home, condo, or villa measuring at least 80 sqm. to 110 sqm. You can buy anywhere in Greece, on the mainland or on their islands.

This permit is renewable every five years.

Your spouse and children younger than 21 can get Residency Permits if they meet certain qualifications.

Investment Residency allows you to live and work anywhere in the 34 European Union nations.

You can travel in the 26 Schengen Member Nations and Citizen countries (191) worldwide, and no visa is required.

You may attend there schools and universities in any European Union countries either free or subsidized rates.

There is an excellent health care system in the EU.

If you are buying through a corporation, you must own 100% of the corporation.

If you and your wife are buying through a joint ownership, each partner must invest E250,000.

Have your attorney or consultant confirm current requirements for Greek Residency requirements, because they may have changed.

Spain

You must invest E500,000 in property in Spain to have the right to reside in Spain and travel in Europe.

This does not allow you to work in Spain, nor participate in the benefits of Spanish citizens.

You may apply for Spanish citizenship which allows you to be issued a Spanish Passport.

The golden visa program in Spain is for Residency and not Citizenship.

There is a difference and it is important to note.

A good real estate agent will know the difference.

New Zeland

You must invest a minimum of 1.5 million in N.Z, for 4 years.

You must have a minimum of 3 years business expeience.

You must have assets of at least N.Z $1,000,000.

You cannot be older than sixty-five years.

You must be able to read and write English.

You have to live in New Zeland at least 164 days for the last 3 years of the 4 year investment period.

There must be evidence that your funds are free and clear, were acquired legally, and are transferrable through the banking system.

In the Investor Plus Visa Program you must invest 10 million in NZD for 3 years.

Family may sponsor a partner, dependent child or parent.

Refugee Family Support has 300 annual slots.

Samoan Quota. A number of citizens of Samoa are invited to live in NZ every year.

Pacific Access Quota. A number of Kirbati, Tuvalu, and Tonga citizens are invited annually.

Mexico

Dual Nationality as reported by the US Embassy & Consulates in Mexico:

"Being a dual national and carrying the passport of another country is perfectly legal. Under US law, naturalizing as a citizen of a foreign state will not in and of itself cause you to lose your US citizenship. General information is available here."

This means available from the U.S Embassy & Consulates in Mexico. You can Google this site.

The Secretaria de Relaciones Exteriores (SRE) manages the naturalization process.

Mexican nationality can be acquired by meeting various residency, cultural integration, or marriage requirements.

Contact the SRE main office for more information.

U.S. Embassy & Consulates in Mexico
Visas
U.S.Citizen-Services
Relationships
Business
Education
Culture
News
Events
Privacy
Sitemap

Costa Rica

To live in Costa Rica for an extended time (over 90 days) you must establish legal residency.

Perpetual Tourism is not allowed. This was a practice of staying for 90 days, leaving for a few days and returning, etc. This practice is being watched. Those doing this may not be allowed to reenter Costa Rica.

If you want to work in Costa Rica you will need a form of residency that allows you to do so.

You should apply for Permanent Residency, or you could be departed and not allowed to re-enter.

You can gain legal residency if you have a lifetime pension (pensionado) guaranteeing income of at least $1,000 US per month.

A rentista is a foreigner with a guaranteed income stream, or who can deposit in a Costa Rica bank at least $60,000 US. It will be paid back to the rentista at $2,500 per month for 24 months. This residency is for 2 years and if you do not deposit another $60,000 you have to leave the country.

If you are an investor with at least $200,000 invested in Costa Rica.

You must enroll in the local CCSS Government Health program known as CAJA.

There are other restrictions and it is best that you contact the Costa Rica Embassy and get the current requirements, and hire someone fluent in Spanish if you are not.

I have visited Costa Rica and found the reception to be warm and friendly. Some of the roads leading out of the major cities are dirt and not smooth, but the climate is wonderful, and there are many Americans living there and going to school there.

RAISE Act

Reforming American Immigration for Strong Employment Act.

As of this writing it does not look like this will pass in the House or Senate of the United States Congress.

However, if it does, here is what RAISE means.

There will be a 50% reduction in annual immigration over 10 years.

This means allotting 539,958 immigrants in 2027 compared to 1,051,031 in 2015.

The diversity visa will be limited to 50,000 per year.

You will have to check on this status yourself to see if the bill passes and if it affects you.

The "feedback" that I am hearing is that it will not pass.

John Stuart Watkins   Resume 2017

Real Estate Experience:
Past President Alaska Multiple Listing Service
Past President Anchorage Board of Realtors
Past Vice President of Realtor's Land Institute
Member Arizona Association of Realtors
Member Tucson Association of Realtors
Past President Tucson Real Estate Exchangors (TREE)
Past President Arizona Property Exchangors (APEX)
Associate Broker Centra Realty in Tucson, AZ

Real Estate Designations:
Graduate Realtor's Land Institute
National Association of Realtor's E-PRO
Certified Webographer

Education:
B. Ed University of Alaska Fairbanks
Master of Arts in Teaching Pacific University Anchorage, Alaska
Endorsed in Special Education, University of Alaska, Anchorage
Endorsed in Gifted Education, University of Alaska, Anchorage

Military Service:
Major in the United States Army, Infantry; Honorable Discharge.

Awards:
National Military High School Smallbore Rifle Champion 1959
Four Time All American University of Alaska Fairbanks Rifle Team
National Collegiate Smallbore Rifle Champion 1963
National Collegiate Large Bore Rifle Champion 1963
National Air Rifle Champion 1969
Gold Medal Winner USA Rifle Team, Cali, Columbia, SA 1971
University of Alaska Fairbanks Athlete Hall of Fame 2010

Memberships:
Life Member National Education Association
Life Member National Rifle Association
Life Member Military Marksmanship Unit
Poetry Society of Virginia
Poetry Society of Arizona
SaddleBrooke Writer's Club
Society of Southwestern Authors
President of the Tucson Poetry Society

Published:

Arizona: 100 Years, 100 Poems, 100 Poets in celebration of Arizona's 100th year of Statehood.

Black and White are only Shades of Gray, or so they say. Personal stories, poems and memoirs.

The House that Ran Away. A book to be read to children or grandchildren.

Kona, Hawaii, Walking Alii Drive. A picture book of hidden treasures few tourists see in Kona.

Oracle, Arizona. Sites to see, places to visit, things to do.

Mommy, Read us a Story. A children's book filled with stories to delight youngsters.

Short Stories to Stimulate, Excite, and Make you Smile

Arizona Poet: Stuart Watkins. A collection of his best poems; some published, and some yet to be published. A good read.

If you want information on a nation that was not covered in this book, or if you would like a referral to a company that specializes in working with persons interested in buying citizenship or residency in the nation of your choice, send me your contact information at:

Arizona Sunshine, LLC
John Stuart Watkins
36251 S. Golf Course Drive
Tucson, AZ 85739
USA
watkins4az@gmail.com